Girl, You Got This!

(A JOURNAL TO IMPROVE LIFE'S IMPERFECTIONS)

Written By: Aganda Gathright, BA, MS

Who Are You?

I'll go first. I'm a woman who was broken, a control freak, depressed, angry, bitter, lonely, a hot mess living life on the edge, but I'm proud to say I didn't allow my past to define my future. I didn't allow my life circumstances to stop my daily progression. I've faced some hard circumstances in my life, and sometimes trying to encourage myself was difficult, but it needed to be done. Today, I am strong, confident, ambitious, loving, kind, hardworking, prosperous, focused, and unshakable. By living without regret and leaning on God to direct me, I kickstarted the process of my healing and thriving. I want the same for you!

I AM A WOMAN THAT:

Used to be afraid of

Loves

Has a goal of

Is driven by

Believes in

Is disappointed by

Would give

Has faith in

Will become one day

AM I HAPPY WITH MYSELF AT THIS TIME?

TEN THINGS THAT MAKE ME WHO I AM:

TEN THINGS I AM NOT DEFINED BY:

t was difficult to finish strong while working through my faults, imperfections, and personal disappointments. IT'S A PROCESS. The process is not easy, but it's ewarding. It may require sacrifices, tears, and even walking away from people, places, or hings in order to becoming the best version of yourself. Through it all, I want you to know... Girl, you got this!

Girl, You Got This - AFFIRMATIONS

I accept myself. I am enough. I love who I am becoming. I am proud of my culture, upbringing, and experiences. They made me who I am.

Relationships

The first big relationship in anyone's life is the relationship with their parents. Unfortunately for me, both of my parents were not active in my life due to drug addiction. As a child, the only healthy relationships I could form were with my grandparents and my maternal aunt and uncle. Growing up fatherless and with a mother who was being physically, emotionally, and mentally abused, I learned at a very young age what to avoid in any relationship. But as I got older, my mother's dark past affected my decision-making when it came to having relationships with men. Eventually, I came to my senses and realized I'm not my mother. I had the opportunity to change my story and live my truth for the better. That is when I allowed God to be the first love of my life. Trust me, girl, God is your first and last love, and He will never leave you, let you down, or bring you harm. I have experienced His love, and it's AMAZING!

HEALTHY RELATIONSHIP/ UNHEALTHY RELATIONSHIP/ HOW TO MOVE ON

What is my definition of self-love?

Who taught me self-love?

Five ways I want to be loved:

What do I want in a relationship at this moment?

What type of relationships/friendships do I want to nourish in my life?

Is my current relationship healthy or toxic?

When you read my story, you may feel bad for me. Girl, don't! My past did hurt, but my present is better because I chose to improve it each day that God gives me breath to start each journey with a purpose. Again, it's a process. Don't allow what you've been through to determine your destiny. I don't look like what I've been through. Trust me, you can too!

Girl, You Got This - AFFIRMATIONS

I am enough. I am worthy of love and deserve to receive love and abundance. I open my heart to love and know that I deserve it. Love surrounds me and everyone around me.

MESSAGE BIBLE:

1 Corinthians 10 :13 - No test or temptation that comes your way is beyond the course of what others have had to face. All you need to remember is that God will never let you down; He'll never let you be pushed past your limit; He'll always be there to help you come through it.

Work & Life Balance

I learned work/life balance in high school when I started my first job. I had to learn how to manage school and work life at a young age. I'm glad I started early because it prepared me for college and my future careers. Trying to manage a full school load, working full-time, paying bills, dealing with horrible men, and juggling other distractions was very difficult. It brought on more stress than I could handle. Girl, have you ever had that inexperience?

WHAT IS MY WORK/LIFE BALANCE STORY? HOW DID I JUGGLE SUCH A CRAZY LIFE? DID IT MAKE ME STRONGER?

What makes me strong?

Why do I struggle with relinquishing control?

What is my life's work?

Girl, You Got This - AFFIRMATIONS

I have everything I need to create new opportunities. I welcome the balance of work and self-care. I am comfortable allowing my light to shine in all situations. I embrace the greatness in me. I bring something unique to the table by simply being me. My time is valuable, and I use it wisely.

MESSAGE BIBLE:

PSALMS 46: 1 – God is a safe place to hide, ready to help when we need him.

From Surviving to Thriving

In my life, I had to become another person to survive all the pain and heartache I endured. I was defensive, hard, mean, callous, untrusting, cautious, guarded, and ready to fight or cuss someone out by any means necessary. I was just surviving, and that kept me from being great and reaching my highest potential. When I learned how to be disciplined in my mind, body and soul, I started to leave those negative things behind me. I learned to look forward to a time where I didn't just survive—I thrived. Girl, the center of bringing any dream into fruition is self-discipline. With success comes struggle. Don't let the struggle break you. No more living with excuses. GIRL, YOU'RE DOING THIS FOR YOU AND YOU GOT THIS!

WHAT ARE THINGS I MUST DISCIPLINE IN MY LIFE?

....

....

....

....

....

....

....

....

....

....

....

....

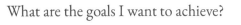

What are the goals I want to achieve?

What layers do I need to pull back in order to bloom?

Who do I need to forgive to tap into my emotional freedom, and healing?

How can self-forgiveness take shape in my life?

Am I ready to let go of just surviving and learn to thrive?

Girl, You Got This – AFFIRMATIONS

My mistakes do not define me or dictate my future success. I am free to evolve and release anything that takes away from my personal growth. Today and every day, I choose to be a radiant light.

Stop Being Everyone's 911!

I have always felt the need to put other people's needs before my own. Girl! I just couldn't say no to anyone. I always felt the need to go above and beyond for others and do the bare minimum for myself. I became so overwhelmed and tired of neglecting myself that my mental health was affected. But girl, guess what? A light went on, and I decided enough was enough. It's okay to say no. It's perfectly fine to say no more. It's okay to guard my heart, mind, and soul. I had to stop focusing on everyone's opinion of me and rely on what God made me to be. God made us each of us unique individuals. We are God's masterpieces, made in his image and called to live out our God–given identity as His children. Never let anyone or anything make you feel guilty for choosing your peace over stress. I had to do what was best for me, because at the end of the day all I have is me. With God giving me strength, nothing is impossible.

What qualities do I need in a support system?

Who in my life can I lean on when things get challenging?

Why can't I say no?

Five ways I can start living on my own terms:

HOW TO CREATE A "NO" MINDSET:

1. Improve your confidence

2. Build stronger boundaries

3. Don't be afraid to say NO

4. Don't feel guilty for prioritizing you first

Girl, You Got This – AFFIRMATIONS

I am deserving of respect. I protect my energy by making myself a priority. I make self-care a priority because it's essential for self-love. My voice matters, and I am confident to speak up in the right moments.

MESSAGE BIBLE:

PHILIPPIANS 4:13 – Whatever I have, wherever I am, I can make it through anything in the One who makes me who I am.

Putting an End To Being a Victim and Becoming a Victor

In life, I have had many situations where I was a victim of my past. But I could not stay in a victimization mindset because it was mentally and emotionally killing me. After being molested, physically abused, neglected as a child, and losing my career, I became a victim of depression, anxiety, PTSD, paranoia, and isolation. Girl, let me tell you this—with prayer and really seeking God's face, I realized I was made in His image. God did not make any mistakes with my life. I had to confess and decree that I was more than enough, that no weapon formed against me shall prosper, and that I can do all things through Christ who strengthens me. I utilized a top-secret weapon called THERAPY. Therapy has changed my life for the better—mentally, physically, and emotionally. It leads to changes that enhance healthy behavior, whether that means improving relationships, expressing emotions better, forgiving self and others, doing better at work or school, or thinking more positively. Therapy became an essential part of my healing. Just know this.... YOU are more than enough to push through any obstacle, girl! God got you!

What are my victories in life? How have they made me a better woman?

What soothes my soul when life is chaotic?

In what ways am I strengthening the bond I have with myself?

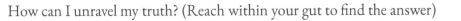

How can I unravel my truth? (Reach within your gut to find the answer)

What is my path in life and how can I start walking on it?

Do I need therapy? (Be honest with yourself)

Girl, You Got This - AFFIRMATIONS

I allow my faith to steer me in the right direction. No weapon formed against me shall prosper. My goals are worth accomplishing. Success is coming to me through the right opportunities. I am energized and ready to slay anything that comes my way.

Girl, It's Your Turn To Shine
(THE POINT OF YOUR TRANSFORMATION)

Say this with me:
I CAN, I WILL, and I MUST!

Jump on your feet and shout it out loud for the world to hear.
I CAN, I WILL, and I MUST!

You can do it, and you WILL do it! You are wonderful, smart, confident, ambitious, courageous, and beautiful inside and out. You are not a quitter; you are a go-getter. You choose to be great and not average. You choose life and not death.

Like the Bible says, walk by faith and not by sight. You are ready to go for your dreams and conquer your fears and failures. It's transformation time.
Say it with me: it's transformation time!

Don't let your past define your future. Don't worry about what others think of you. Their opinions mean nothing. You have survived the storm; you have endured your mistakes and bad choices. It's your time.

GIRL, YOU GOT THIS!

MESSAGE BIBLE:

ROMANS 12: 2 – Don't become so well-adjusted to your culture that you fit into it without even thinking; instead, fix your attention on God. You'll be changed from the inside out. Readily recognize what he wants from you, and quickly respond to it. Unlike the culture around you, always dragging you down to its level of immaturity, God brings the best out of you and develops well-informed maturity in you.

Vision Board

LOVE:

HEALTH:

CAREER:

FAMILY:

FINANCES:

FUN:

MENTAL/EMOTIONAL STABILITY:

Girl You Got This!
Vision Board

THINGS TO CHANGE:

Girl You Got This!
Vision Board

NEXT BIG GOALS:

References

BibleGateway. (2008). 1 Corinthians 10:13 (MSG). https://www.biblegateway.com/passage/?search=1%20Corinthians%2010%3A13&version=MSG

BibleGateway. (2008). Psalm 46:1–3 (MSG). https://www.biblegateway.com/passage/?search=Psalm%2046%3A1&version=MSG

BibleGateway. (2008c). Romans 12:2 (MSG). https://www.biblegateway.com/passage/?search=ROMANS+12%3A2&version=MSG

BibleStudyTools Staff. (2014). Philippians 4:13. Biblestudytools.Com. https://www.biblestudytools.com/msg/philippians/4-13.html

CPSIA information can be obtained
at www.ICGtesting.com
Printed in the USA
BVHW050053310122
627600BV00007B/366